# of Imani
Celebration of Women

By Tamara Lewis

Editor: Marilyn E. Thornton
Cover Design/Illustration: Keely Moore

05 06 07 08 09 10 11 12 13 14—10 9 8 7 6 5 4 3 2 1

Contents

Lisa Williamson (Sister Souljah)

Lisa Williamson, otherwise known as Sister Souljah, was born in the Bronx, New York in 1964, into a family that was soon embroiled in the dehumanizing system of public welfare. Williamson was an extremely talented student. While still in high school, Lisa became a legislative intern in the House of Representatives for the Republican Party. Later, she won the American Legion's Constitutional Oratory Contest. After attending Cornell University's advanced placement summer program and the University of Salamanca's study-abroad program in Spain, she went on to attend Rutgers University. There, she became a well-known writer and political commentator for the university's newspaper.

While Lisa was at Rutgers University, Reverend Benjamin Chavis of The United Church of Christ Commission for Racial Justice offered her a job. In this capacity she developed the African Survival Camp, a three-year summer camp program for homeless families. She received her degree in American History and African Studies.

As a hip-hop artist, Sister Souljah incorporated her views concerning injustice toward Black Americans in her music. Her 1992 rap album, *360 Degrees of Power,* combines her thoughts and personal and professional experience. Her mode of communication may be shrill to some but real to others.

Sister Souljah traveled and lectured all over America, Europe, and Africa and has volunteered in a medical center in Mozambique and refugee camps in Zimbabwe. She also spoke at the Million Women March in Philadelphia. A teacher of history and current events, Williamson educates teenagers about womanhood, manhood, and teen pregnancy. Her books include *No Disrespect* and national bestseller *The Coldest Winter Ever*.

Currently, Sister Souljah is Executive Director of Daddy's House Social Programs, a non-profit organization for children that rap artist Sean Puffy Combs established. The program serves 600 children from ages six to sixteen from the streets of New York, New Jersey, and Philadelphia, aiming to help poor, homeless, and abused children.

Sister Souljah proclaims that the United States' public education system has systematically denied African Americans the right to study and enjoy their culture and history. Further, she argues that Black Americans are neglected politically, economically, and internationally in the areas of economic development and social policy. In her writings, teachings, and leadership, she is working to bring attention to these injustices.

Sister Souljah

"But Souljah won't hide. I won't hide because the Bible says to whom much is given, much is expected, and I already told you I was blessed with spiritual eyes."

From *No Disrespect*

8

Maya Angelou

Maya Angelou was born Marguerite Johnson on April 4, 1928. She spent most her early childhood with her grandmother in segregated Stamps, Arkansas. After eighth grade, she moved to San Francisco to live with her mother. In high school, she won a scholarship in dance and drama at the California Labor School. Later, Angelou went on to become San Francisco's first Black American streetcar conductor. In the early 1950s, she married a Greek American former sailor, Tosh Angelos. She took a variation of his name as her stage name in her work as a dancer and singer of West Indian calypso music in San Francisco and New York.

Maya Angelou spent several years touring Europe in the musical *Porgy and Bess* before returning to New York and joining the Harlem Writers Guild. She then traveled to Egypt, working as associate editor for the Cairo-based *Arab Observer,* an English-language weekly. During the regime of Kwame Nkrumah, she moved on to Accra, Ghana, where she was a featured editor of *The African Review.* She also taught music and drama at the University of Ghana. Next, she went on to Sweden, where she studied cinematography.

In 1970 Maya published *I Know Why the Caged Bird Sings,* the first volume of her autobiography. This book became the basis for a two-hour TV special on CBS. She has written and produced several prize-winning documentaries, including the PBS special *Afro-Americans in the Arts,* for which she received the Golden Eagle Award.

In 1971 she was nominated for a Pulitzer Prize for her first volume of poetry, entitled *Just Give Me a Cool Drink of Water 'fore I Diiie.* The same year, Maya wrote the screenplay and musical score for the film *Georgia, Georgia,* becoming the first Black woman to have an original screenplay produced. Blues artist B.B. King has even recorded some of her musical compositions. In addition to her musical accomplishments, Angelou was nominated for an Emmy Award for her acting in the miniseries *Roots.* Maya is fluent in French, Spanish, Italian, and West African Fanti.

Her book of essays *Wouldn't Take Nothing for My Journey Now* is dedicated to Oprah Winfrey, who claims Maya Angelou as one of her mentors. At the request of President-elect Clinton, she wrote and delivered a poem "On the Pulse of Morning," for his inauguration in 1993.

Maya Angelou lectures throughout the US and abroad and teaches American Studies at Wake Forest University in North Carolina.

Maya Angelou

"If we persist in self-disrespect and then ask our children to respect themselves, it is as if we break all their bones and then insist that they win Olympic gold medals for the hundred-yard dash."

From *Wouldn't Take Nothing for My Journey Now*

11

12

Sojourner Truth

Sojourner Truth was born a slave in Ulster County, New York, in 1797. Her given name was Isabella Baumfree. Her mother was called "Mau-mau Bett." As one of the youngest of ten to twelve children, Isabella was spared from being sold away. In the evenings, Mau-mau Bett taught Isabella about a God who heard their prayers and offered protection and healing from the hard things in life. Mau-mau Bett also gave Isabella lessons in ethics, telling her daughter to always tell the truth, to refrain from stealing, and to be obedient.

Isabella's first owners were Dutch. Upon the death of her master when she was nine, she was separated from her parents and sold to a family that spoke only English. She had to learn English fast or be whipped. Until that time she had spoken only Dutch.

Later, she married Thomas, one of her master's slaves, and had five children with him. Although slaves could be sold only in state, Isabella's son Peter had been illegally sold and sent to Alabama. Many in the White community could not understand all the fuss she was making over "a little nigger," as her former mistress called her son. But Isabella was determined to have her child. In 1826, with the help of Quakers, she secured the return of her son, even though she was not yet legally free. Sources indicate that Isabella tried to help Black mothers in Washington, D.C., file suit for children stolen and sold into slavery.

Although the state of New York ended slavery in 1827, her master had refused to let her go. So Isabella "walked away in broad daylight," as she describes it, to take hold of her freedom. Isabella then worked as a maid and cook in various homes.

Isabella had the habit of going off by herself to commune with God. She would create a personal chapel of tree limbs and leaves on a small island in a stream. One day she was so inspired and strengthened by her new relationship with God that she heard the call to preach. She changed her name to Sojourner Truth, meaning "one who travels and spreads the truth." Then she went from place to place, preaching the Word of God and talking about the evils of slavery and the mistreatment of women. Although she had never been taught to read, she preached as inspired by the Spirit; one of her favorite topics was "When I Found Jesus." In 1850, her memoirs, entitled, *The Narrative of Sojourner Truth,* were published.

Sojourner Truth fought for the desegregation of public transportation in Washington, D.C., during the Civil War. She brought a local street to a standstill when a driver refused her passage. With the backing of the crowd, she forced the driver to carry her. She also supported the Black soldiers who fought in the Civil War, speaking before Congress and two presidents. Additionally, she fought for the rights and of all women in the feminist and suffragist movements.

Her most famous speeches indicate her passionate defense of women. In 1851, Sojourner Truth attended a women's rights conference in Akron, Ohio, to sell her autobiography. After one day of listening to male ministers use the Bible to put women down and deny them of equal rights, Sojourner's uninvited rebuttal speech silenced the crowd. She told of her experiences in life, showing that while she was strong enough to do the work of a man, she was a woman, who no one ever pampered or put on a pedestal. When her children were sold into slavery, no one but Jesus heard her cries.

In 1858, when pro-slavery persons at a meeting in Indiana derisively declared that she must be a man, Sojourner opened her blouse and bared her breasts, asking if anyone wanted to nurse. In her strength, Sojourner claimed her womanhood and demanded that all women be viewed as equals to men.

Nana (Mother) Yaa Asantewaa

Nana (Mother) Yaa Asantewaa was born in 1863. She was the queen of Ejisu, part of the Ashanti Kingdom, which King Osei Tutu I had founded in the seventeenth century. The kingdom was located in the heart of Central Ghana's forest, in West Africa. The priest of the kingdom, Okomfo Anokye, declared that the soul of the new nation could be found in the Ashanti Golden Stool. Tradition has it that this stool had fallen from the sky and landed in the lap of the king.

Since 1805, the Ashanti people had been at war with the British colonial forces. In 1896, the British finally captured and exiled the Asantehene, or king. Four years later, the governor of the British army insulted the Ashanti people by demanding that they give him the Golden Stool so that he could sit on it. As the Queen Mother of Esiju, Yaa Asantewaa called on the men of Ashanti to fight for their king, their homeland, and their honor. Otherwise, she said, the women would do so until none were left standing. By her words, she inspired the warriors to stand up for their honor and heritage.

Nana Yaa Asantewaa led the kingdom as Supreme Commander, and the nine-month war came to be known as the Yaa Asantewaa War. The British resorted to unscrupulous tactics and captured Yaa Asantewaa and other Ashanti leaders, whose deportation to the Seychelles Islands brought the war to an end. Nana Yaa Asantewaa died in exile in 1921. Nevertheless, she became a legendary figure and national hero in Ghanaian history. She is the only woman featured on the national currency of Ghana.

18

Marian Wright Edelman

Marian Wright (later Edelman) was born in South Carolina in 1939, the youngest of five children of a Baptist minister. Her parents expected their children to get an education and serve the community. Her father believed that if you had no homework, you should assign yourself something to do. He set high goals for his children, naming his youngest after Marian Anderson.

Marian Wright Edelman attended Spelman College in Atlanta, Georgia. She won a Charles Merrill grant and with it studied abroad for a year, first at Sorbonne University in Paris, France, and then at the University of Geneva in Switzerland. Awarded a Lisle Fellowship, she studied for two months in the Soviet Union. Upon her return to the segregated society of the South, Marian became intensely involved in the civil rights movement. In 1960, she graduated from Spelman as the valedictorian and was accepted into Yale University Law School as a John Hay Whitney Fellow.

During law school, Marian continued her involvement in Mississippi's struggle for freedom. She became one of the first two interns for the NAACP's Legal Defense and Educational Fund in 1963 and established its office in Jackson, Mississippi. From 1964–68, she headed this office. Marian went on to become the first Black woman admitted to the Mississippi bar. She brought Robert F. Kennedy, who was at the time a New York senator, to Mississippi so that he could see firsthand the homes of the poor. Her strategy effectively drew attention to the problem of hunger and the need for federal help in the form of food stamps. At this point, Marian began to realize that in order to more effectively create change, she needed to be in a position to affect federal policy.

She moved to Washington, D.C., and worked with Martin Luther King, Jr. to plan the Poor People's March on Washington, which took place after his death. Soon afterward, she founded the Children's Defense Fund, which aims to "leave no child behind" and to ensure every child a healthy, fair, safe, and moral start in life. Through the CDF, she organized the Stand for Children March, which drew more than 200,000 people to Washington in June, 1996, and brought attention to the needs of disadvantaged Americans of all colors. Under Marian's leadership, the CDF has become a strong national voice for children and families.

Marian has won many honorary degrees and awards, including the Presidential Medal of Freedom, the nation's highest civilian award, and the Robert F. Kennedy Lifetime Achievement Award for her writings. Her five books include *Families in Peril: An Agenda For Social Change,* the number-one New York Times bestseller *The Measure of Our Success: A Letter to My Children and Yours, Guide My Feet: Meditations and Prayers on Loving and Working for Children,* and *Lanterns: A Memoir of Mentors.*

Marian Wright Edelman

"[Our elders] taught us to be neither victims nor victimizers; they urged us not to hate White folks because God created White folks and Black folks and Brown folks and all folks out of the same dust and would hold us—and them—ultimately to the same standards of justice."

From *Guide My Feet*

21

Clara Hale

Clara McBride Hale, known as Mother Hale, was the founder of Hale House, a temporary home for abandoned and drug-addicted babies and young children. She was born on April 1, 1905, in North Carolina and grew up in Philadelphia, Pennsylvania. The youngest of four children, she was raised by her mother when her father died.

Clara married Thomas Hale and moved to New York City, where she cleaned houses and theaters. They had two children. When her husband died of cancer while their children were still young, she started a home child-care facility so that she would be able to supervise her own children. This job included taking in foster children, many of whom preferred her home to theirs. By the time she retired in 1968, Mother Hale had raised forty foster children, and all of them pursued a college education.

In 1969, Mother Hale began to take in sick babies who had inherited their mothers' drug addiction. Hale's own adult children provided the first funds to support the addicted babies. In 1970, the city of New York began funding the Hale House, which moved to a five-story brownstone in 1975. The babies remained at Hale House until their mothers completed a drug rehabilitation program.

Mother Hale showed love and nurture to the children. She would give them a great deal of affection, making sure they were well-fed and nurtured. She refused to give them drug medications that would alleviate the symptoms of withdrawal, believing that doing so would only prolong the healing process and increase the physical need for drugs.

As their small bodies struggled to get all the drugs out of their system, Mother Hale would walk and talk with them as they cried and suffered. She would tell them how beautiful they were and that she expected them to get an education. Mother Hale whispered in theirs ears that they should be proud to be Black, proud of their Black brothers and sisters, and that they should learn to pull together. She believed that all Black children could become persons of substance and worth if they only made up their minds to do so.

Since 1969, Hale House has been home to hundreds of babies whose parents are dealing with drug addiction. Her work was recognized by President Ronald Reagan. In 1985's State of the Union Address, he called her an "American hero." In June of the same year, Clara Hale received an honorary Doctorate of Humane Letters degree from the John Jay College of Criminal Justice. In 1990, she received the Booth Community Service Award, the highest award from the Salvation Army. When Mother Hale died in 1992, her daughter Lorraine Hale, Ph.D., who had worked by her side for twenty-five years, became Executive President and CEO of Hale House. The organization continues to offer life-changing refuge and comfort for drug-addicted babies.

Mother Clara Hale

"Being black does not stop you. . . . You can have anything you want if you make up your mind and you want it."

From *Epic Lives,* edited by Jessie Carney Smith

Mary McLeod Bethune

Mary McLeod Bethune (1875–1955) was born near Mayesville, South Carolina, the fifteenth child of former slaves. Her father was of African and Native American descent, and her mother was of African descent. Although she did not begin school until the age of ten, Mary had a great thirst for education. She attended Trinity Presbyterian Mission School when it opened in 1885, and she received scholarships that enabled her to continue her education at Scotia Seminary in Concord, North Carolina.

In addition to academics, these missionary institutions emphasized religion, "culture and refinement," and "industrial education," which included sewing, cooking, laundering, and cleaning. In the segregated South, this curriculum served the needs of what was available for young Black women, enabling them to be employable in upscale settings, such as classrooms. Bethune, however, sought to be a missionary to Africa and enrolled in the Bible Institute for Home and Foreign Missions (later the Moody Bible Institute) in Chicago. When the Presbyterian Mission Board turned her down for the job on the basis of her race, Mary turned to teaching.

By 1900, Mary had married and had established her first school, a Presbyterian parochial school in Palatka, Florida.

Two years later, she opened an independent school. In 1904 she moved to Daytona and opened the Daytona Educational and Industrial Institute "with five little girls, a dollar and a half, and faith in God," as Mary described it. Using the model of Scotia Seminary, Bethune hoped to build an institution that would eventually offer nursing and gain national credibility. Mary proved to be an able fundraiser, gaining support from local churches, wealthy Whites in the area, and corporate donations from philanthropists such as James M. Gamble, founder of Proctor & Gamble.

In 1923 the Daytona Normal and Industrial Institute merged with Cookman Institute in Jacksonville, Florida, a school with Methodist Episcopal sponsorship. In 1929, the school was named Bethune-Cookman College. Under Mary's leadership, it survived the worst of the Great Depression, and in 1935, the NAACP awarded her the Spingarn Medal for that achievement.

As she built the college, she used it to develop the movement of women's clubs, whose state and regional meetings were hosted at the school. In 1920 Mary became president of the Southeastern Association of Colored Women, and from 1924-1928 she served as president of the National Association of Colored Women, an organization of ten thousand women. Because she believed that Black women should be able to affect national affairs, she founded the National Council of Negro Women in New York City in 1935.

In 1936, Mary accepted a full-time position in Washington, D.C., that developed into the directorship of the Division of

Negro Affairs for the National Youth Administration in 1939. She facilitated the organization the Federal Council on Negro Affairs, known as the Black Cabinet, which helped establish and carry out government programs that assisted Blacks.

During the 1930s and 1940s, Mary used to her contacts in the Franklin Roosevelt administration, her friendship with his wife, Eleanor, and her organizational skills to garner a piece of the New Deal pie for African Americans. She also nurtured the NCNW so that it included professional, occupational, educational, and social organizations and eighty-two metropolitan councils. Mary's work in FDR's Democratic government helped cause a shift in the political affiliations of many Black Americans, most of whom had retained membership in the party of Abraham Lincoln, who was a Republican. Today, a statue near Capitol Hill in Washington, D.C. commemorates her legacy.

Kentake Amanerinas of Meroe

From 542 B.C. to 350 A.D., the Meroes ruled Nubia, a region in southern Egypt and northern Sudan. During this period, many Kentakes, or Queen Mothers, ruled over Nubia. The Kentake was the source of the royal right to office, and she was said to embody the people's wisdom as the preserver of the national culture. She directed armies, trade, and diplomatic relations, and she played a prominent role in the choice and coronation of the new king.

During the Meriotic period of the Nubian Empire, the queen mother ruled in her own right, and, according to tradition, the succession of power passed down through her daughter or daughter-in-law. It is believed that during the Meriotic period of the history of Nubia, only queens ruled. Four of these queens—Amanerinas, Amanishakhete, Nawidemak and Maleqereabar—became distinctively known as Candaces, a corruption of the word *kentake*.

Amanirenas was a Kentake who ruled Nubia during the reign of the first emperor of Rome, Augustus Caesar. Sources indicate that she was friends and ally with the Egyptian

Queen Cleopatra. However, since Cleopatra knew she was no military match for the Romans, she tried to seduce the Roman general Marc Antony in order to maintain power (and failed). The Nubian Kentake Amanirenas would use no such devices. Instead, she militarily defended her country and kept Rome out of Nubia forever.

The classical writings of the Greek historian Strabo describe a military clash between the Romans and the Nubians during the reign of Augustus Caesar. In 22 B.C., after Cleopatra had died and the Romans had invaded Egypt, the Roman military was moving south to take over Nubia. Rather than wait for the Romans to attack her country, Kentake Amanerinas took the offensive, invading Roman colonies to the north in Egypt and on the Nubian frontier.

The Roman leader, Petronius, tried to fight the army of Kentake Amanerinas but was held off by Nubian power, and the clash resulted in a standoff. Finally, Nubian ambassadors negotiated a peace treaty with Augustus Caesar. Although the peace treaty promised tribute to be paid by the Meroites to the Romans, tribute was never paid. The Romans retreated as far as Egypt. Although the Romans had conquered Egypt, the Nubian Kentake Amanerinas, through military power, diplomatic prowess, and iron will, refused to let the Romans conquer Nubia.

Kentake Amanerinas of Meroe

"It is likely that Candace did not return all the statues of Caesar which the Ethiopians had torn down, for a splendid head of Augustus, apparently buried ceremonially as an important trophy, was discovered at excavations at Meroe."

From *Blacks in Antiquity,* by Frank Snowden

33

34

Mary Eliza Mahoney

Mary Eliza Mahoney, born on May 7, 1845, was the first African-American registered nurse in the United States. A child of free parents, Ms. Mahoney was born in in Dorchester, Massachusetts. As a teenager, she became interested in nursing, and she began working at the New England Hospital for Women and Children (now Dimock Community Health Center) in Roxbury, Massachusetts. For fifteen years, she worked as a cook, janitor, washerwoman, and unofficial nurse's assistant.

In 1878, at the age of thirty-three, Mary became a student in the rigorous nursing program of New England Hospital for Women and Children. The program lasted for sixteen months. At the end of this period, she completed the course among a fraction of those who began the program with her. After graduation she became a private-duty nurse, working in hospitals, clinics, and homes for the next thirty years. She finally became director of an orphanage in Long Island, New York.

In 1896, Mary became one of the original members of the Nurses Association, later known as the American Nurses Association, a predominantly White organization. Later, in 1908, she became cofounder of the National Association of Colored Graduate Nurses (NACGN). Mary gave the welcoming address at the association's first convention and served as chaplain for the NACGN. She remained active in the ANA, the NACGN, and other affiliated organizations until her death in 1926. In 1976, Mahoney was inducted into the Nursing Hall of Fame.

Faye Wattleton

Faye Wattleton was born on July 8, 1943, in St. Louis, Missouri. She earned a B.S. in Nursing from Ohio State University and an M.S. in Maternal and Infant Care, with certification as a nurse-midwife, from Columbia University. She is currently the president of the Center for Gender Equality, a research, policy-development, and educational institution devoted to advancing women's equality. The Center for Gender Equality works in conjunction with other educational institutions, studying socio-economic issues of women in order to make recommendations to policy-makers at the local, state, and national levels of government. The organization also uses its research to solicit governmental and private corporate funding for specific causes concerning the rights and welfare of women.

Faye Wattleton has also served as president of the Planned Parenthood Federation, the nation's oldest voluntary reproductive health organization. During her administration, Planned Parenthood experienced a period of growth caused by restructuring the national office, increasing the operating budget, expanding the program internationally, and developing a national advocacy program. Her work enabled

Planned Parenthood to become the country's seventh largest charity, providing medical and educational services to four million Americans a year.

Faye has been prominent in the national debate over reproductive rights and health. She has received several awards and was inducted into the National Women's Hall of Fame in 1993. Her memoir, *Life on the Line,* was published in 1996. She has been featured in a variety of national publications and was voted as one of America's 100 most fascinating African-American women by *Ebony* magazine in 1999.

Faye Wattleton holds twelve honorary degrees and presently serves on the boards of directors of the Empire Blue Cross & Blue Shield, Estée Lauder Companies, the Quidel Corporation, Bio-Technology General, The Henry J. Kaiser Family Foundation, and Jazz at Lincoln Center. She has been a Trustee of the Institute of International Education since 1994.

Faye Wattleton

"There is a major cause for our higher rates of teen pregnancy and childbirth: the fundamental discomfort of Americans with sexuality."

From *The Black Women's Health Book*, edited by Evelyn C. White

40

Gbeto Warriors

Gbeto warriors were a terrifying division of female soldiers in the Dahomean army in the 1700s and 1800s. Recruited from among the healthiest and strongest young women, these females were sworn to chastity and allegiance to the king. They were thoroughly trained to overcome pain by enduring physical hardships and doing gymnastics. Organized and trained to fight with passion, Gbeto warriors used muskets, machetes, swords, and their bare teeth.

The Gbeto served as the king's official bodyguards and held special status as celibate warrior "wives" of the King. These warriors were known for their ruthlessness, eating raw meat, filing their teeth into sharp points, and keeping the jawbones and skulls of their enemies as trophies. They prided themselves on their hardened physiques and highly-trained martial skills, and constantly strove to outperform their male counterparts. The Gbeto became a dynastic tradition, and through consistent military action against nearby kingdoms, they became known as merciless, undefeatable opponents. By 1890 they were a significant portion of the Dahomey fighting force. Because of the Gbeto warriors' military influence, Dahomey became one of the last of the African kingdoms to yield to European colonialism.

Today, young descendants of the Gbeto warriors serve as the king's ceremonial bodyguards in Benin. These pre-adolescent girls dance at the king's court, wielding play swords and axes and singing tales of their ancestors' bloody conquests. Storytellers recount colorful tales of these famous warriors who tore trees out of the ground to use as clubs. Clearly, the memory of these female warriors is still alive.

42

Hilda Hutcherson, M.D.

After graduating with a degree from Harvard Medical School in 1980, Hilda Hutcherson has become an esteemed obstetrician and gynecologist. She is currently a co-director of the New York Center for Women's Sexual Health at Columbia Presbyterian Medical Center. She also works as Assistant Professor of Obstetrics and Gynecology at Columbia University's College of Physicians and Surgeons, and Associate Dean for Diversity and Minority Affairs at Columbia University's College of Physicians and Surgeons. She has practiced gynecology for more than twenty years and serves on the Speaker's Bureau of the Sexuality Information and Education Council of the United States.

Hilda Hutcherson, who is married and has four children, is sought internationally as a consultant and advisor and health on sexuality issues for women. She has been featured on several radio programs, *The Oprah Winfrey Show,* and other television programs. Her recent book, *What Your Mother Never Told You About S-e-x** (2002), offers an exhaustive reference on sex and female sexuality. Hilda offers facts on female and male anatomy, birth control, and more, and in a conversational style, she shows women how they can pass critical information on to their daughters.

*This resource includes chapters that explicitly explore the sexual body, sex acts, sexual health and safety, lifelong sex, and sex problems. It answers questions that women have been afraid to ask about their bodies but need to know to become comfortable with their sexuality—and with sex. Mentors should review this material thoroughly before utilizing it with participants.

Other Resources

• The Center for Disease Control's National AIDS Hotline: 1-800-342-AIDS (2437).

• *Every Young Woman's Battle: Guarding Your Mind, Heart, and Body in a Sex-Saturated World,* by Shannon Ethridge and Stephen Arterburn (WaterBrook Press, 2004; ISBN 1578568560).

• "HIV/AIDS Among African Americans" *(http://www.cdc. gov/hiv/pubs/Facts/afam.htm)*. This website shows the risk factors for African Americans and discusses how to prevent HIV infection.

• "HIV/AIDS Among US Women: Minority and Young Women at Continuing Risk" *(http://www.cdc.gov/hiv/pubs/ facts/women.htm)*. This fact sheet discusses the risk of heterosexual contact for women, as well as prevention needs for young women.

- *Keeping It Real: A Faith-Based Model for Teen Dialogue on Sex & Sexuality™,* curriculum developed by the Black Church Initiative of the Religious Coalition For Reproductive Choice. (For more information, visit *http://www.rcrc.org/ get_involved/black_church_initiative/keeping_it_real.htm.*) The RCRC is located at 1025 Vermont Avenue, N.W., Suite 1103, Washington, D.C., 20005. The RCRC's telephone number is (202) 628-7700, and its website address is *www.rcrc.org.*

- "Primary HIV Infection Associated With Oral Transmission" *(http://www.cdc.gov/hiv/pubs/facts/oralsexqa.htm).* This website has a Q&A format that discusses the risk factors of HIV infection through oral transmission.

- *Sex Has a Price Tag,* by Pam Stenzel and Crystal Kirgiss (Zondervan Publishing Company, 2003; ISBN 0310249716).

46

Dr. Mae Jemison

Mae C. Jemison was born in Decatur, Alabama, on October 17, 1956, and is the youngest of three children. She was raised in Chicago, Illinois. At an early age, Mae developed interests in anthropology, archaeology, and astronomy. She entered college at the age of sixteen and earned degrees in Chemical Engineering and African American Studies from Stanford University in 1977. Mae received a Doctor of Medicine degree from Weill-Cornell College of Medicine in 1981. While in medical school, she traveled to Cuba, Kenya and Thailand, providing primary medical care to people living there.

After medical school, Mae served in the Area Peace Corps as a medical officer in Sierra Leone and Liberia, West Africa. There, she supervised the pharmacy, laboratory, and medical staff. She also provided medical care, wrote self-care manuals, developed and implemented guidelines for health and safety issues for volunteer job-placement and training sites. She also worked in conjunction with the Center for Disease Control (CDC) on research for various vaccines.

After returning from the Peace Corps, Mae served as General Practitioner for CIGNA Health Plans of California in Los Angeles. There, she applied to the National Aeronautics and Space Administration (NASA) for admission to the astronaut program. Her first application was not accepted. On her second try, she was accepted and became one of the fifteen candidates accepted from some 2,000 applicants.

Mae completed the astronaut-training program in 1988, becoming the first Black female astronaut. In August 1992, Jemison went on to become the first Black woman in space. During the mission aboard the space shuttle, she conducted experiments in materials processing and life sciences.

In 1993, Mae Jemison founded the Jemison Group, Inc., which focuses on improving healthcare in Africa. Mae is also Adjunct Professor of Community and Family Medicine at Dartmouth Medical School. She speaks fluent Russian, Japanese, and Swahili, as well as English.

Dr. Mae Jemison

"We can't afford the talent base in this country not to be utilized. It's the right thing that we have people involved."

50

Ida B. Wells-Barnett

Ida Bell Wells (later Barnett) was born in 1862, in Holly Springs, Mississippi, a daughter of slaves. Her parents died when she was a teenager, and she had to teach in order to take care of her brothers and sisters. She became a schoolteacher and was educated at Rust University. From 1884 to 1891, Wells taught in rural schools in Mississippi and Tennessee and attended summer classes at Fisk University, in Nashville, Tennessee.

In 1884, Ida purchased a railroad ticket in Memphis and took a seat in the section reserved for Whites. When the conductor asked her to move, she refused and was physically thrown off the train. She successfully sued the Chesapeake and Ohio Railroad Company for discrimination. Upon appeal, however, the Supreme Court of Tennessee reversed the lower court's ruling.

Ida turned to journalism. Using the pen name Iola, she wrote for newspapers owned by Black Americans, and her articles covered issues such as the education of Black children. She wrote for and acquired ownership of the militant newspaper *Free Speech and Headlight* in Memphis. In her editorials, she denounced the lynching of three personal friends. As a result, the newspaper's office was mobbed and destroyed by local Whites, whereupon Ida began a crusade to investigate the lynching of Black Americans throughout the South.

With a death threat hanging over her head in Memphis, Ida decided to move to Chicago. During this time, she wrote the pamphlet *A Red Record* (1895), a statistical account and analysis of three years of lynching. She subsequently traveled throughout the United States and England, lecturing and founding anti-lynching societies and Black American women's clubs.

In 1893, Ida organized a Black women's civic club in Chicago. She later became one of the founders of the Chicago Negro Fellowship league, which aided newly arrived migrants from the South. She was also a women's rights advocate, starting what may have been the first African-American women's suffrage group. Working with Jane Addams, she successfully blocked the establishment of segregated public schools in Chicago. She also served as a probation officer from 1913 to 1917 for the Chicago municipal court. In 1895 Wells married Ferdinand Lee Barnett, a lawyer who was founder and editor of *The Conservator,* the first Black newspaper in Chicago. Ida B. Wells-Barnett died in 1931.

Ida B. Wells-Barnett

"I have firmly believed all along that the law was on our side and would, when we appealed to it, give us justice. I feel shorn of that belief and utterly discouraged, and just now, if it were possible, would gather my race and fly away with them."

Dr. Condoleezza Rice

Condoleezza Rice was born November 14, 1954, in Birmingham, Alabama. She became a member of Phi Beta Kappa at the University of Denver and graduated cum laude with a degree in political science. She went on to receive a Ph.D. in International Studies from the University of Denver. She served as professor of political science at Stanford University, winning high teaching honors.

Condoleezza is a member of the Center for International Security and Arms Control, the Institute for International Studies, and the Hoover Institution. Among her books are *Germany Unified and Europe Transformed* with Philip Zelikow (1995), *The Gorbachev Era* with Alexander Dallin (1986), and *Uncertain Allegiance: The Soviet Union and the Czechoslovak Army* (1984). She also has written several articles on Soviet and East European foreign and defense policy and has spoken all over the world to audiences about these subjects.

In 1986, she served as international affairs fellow of the Council on Foreign Relations. From 1989 through 1991, she served in the first Bush Administration as Director and Senior Director of Soviet and East European Affairs in the National Security Council. She went on to serve as a Special Assistant to the President for National Security Affairs. Condoleezza has also served as Special Assistant to the Director of the Joint Chiefs of Staff. In 1997, she was on the Federal Advisory Committee on Gender Integrated Training in the Military.

Condoleezza became National Security Advisor in 2001. In 2004, she received a nomination for Secretary of State.

Condoleezza also co-founded the Center for a New Generation, an after-school academy in East Palo Alto, California, and has been on the board of directors for Chevron, the Hewlett Foundation, and Charles Schwab. She has been a member of J.P. Morgan's international advisory council, the Council of Foreign Relations, and the National Endowment for the Humanities trustee board, and is a fellow of the American Academy of Arts and Sciences.

She has been awarded honorary doctorates from Morehouse College, the University of Alabama, the University of Notre Dame, the National Defense University, the Mississippi College School of Law, the University of Louisville, and Michigan State University.

Condoleezza is also a highly accomplished classical pianist.

Condoleezza Rice

"I've always felt you should not see race and gender in everything. You should give people the benefit of the doubt."

Madam C.J. Walker

Madam C.J. Walker was born Sarah Breedlove in 1867, on a cotton plantation in Louisiana. She has been described as the first African-American woman millionaire and as the first self-made American woman millionaire. She was the first American woman who obtained her fortune through her own efforts and not through inheritance.

Sarah Breedlove's parents died when she was seven years old. She married when she was fourteen, but her husband soon died, leaving her with a two-year-old daughter. She then moved to St. Louis and worked as a laundress. Suffering from scalp disease, which was rampant among Black American women in the early 1900s, she sought a cure for the condition. She then decided to start her own line of hair care products.

With the help of Charles Walker, whom she married in 1906, she set up a mail order business in Denver, Colorado. The mail order business flourished, and soon she was traveling all over the country promoting her hair care products. She considered herself to be a hair culturist and taught others how to heal the scalp and stimulate hair growth with her Walker System. The company grew to include offices in Pittsburgh,

Indianapolis, and Harlem as well as a beauty school in Pittsburgh. By 1919, the Walker Company included over 20,000 salespersons and hairdressers in the United States, Central America, and the Caribbean.

Madam Walker was a strong advocate of Black American women's economic independence. She created business opportunities for women at a time when the only other options were domestic work and sharecropping. Having started a multibillion dollar Black cosmetics industry, she used her wealth and status to work toward political and economic rights for African Americans and women. Madam Walker was also a noted philanthropist to the African-American community, contributing thousands of dollars to artists of the Harlem Renaissance, Black American schools, individuals, organizations, and institutions.

Madam C.J. Walker

"I am a woman who came from the cotton fields of the South. From there I was promoted to the washtub. From there I was promoted to the cook kitchen. And from there I promoted myself into the business of manufacturing hair goods and preparations.... I have built my own factory on my own ground."

Madam Walker, 1912,
National Negro Business League Convention

61

Maggie Lena Walker

Maggie Lena Walker, the first woman of any race to become president of a bank, was born July 15, 1867, in Richmond, Virginia. Maggie was the daughter of former slaves and was raised by her mother after the death of her father, who was presumably murdered. Maggie attended the Lancaster School and then the Armstrong Normal School, which trained students to be teachers. Maggie graduated at the age of sixteen and began teaching at the Lancaster School.

In September of 1886, Maggie married Armstead Walker, Jr., a building contractor. They had three sons, one of whom died as an infant. After her teaching career, Maggie became an agent for an insurance company, the Woman's Union.

Since the age of fourteen, Maggie had been a member of the Independent Order of St. Luke, an African-American fraternal and cooperative insurance society that assisted sick and elderly members and paid for burial and funeral services. The order was founded in Baltimore in 1867, by a former slave, Mary Prout. The society had its headquarters in Richmond in 1889.

That year, Maggie was named secretary-treasurer of the Order of St. Luke. Under her leadership, the Order increased its membership greatly by encouraging many other Black

American women to manage and save their money. On behalf of the Order, Maggie expanded its capital, increased its staff, and established the St. Luke Penny Savings Bank, later called the Consolidated Bank and Trust Company. She served as chairman of the board and became the first woman in the United States to direct a bank. This bank still exists in Richmond today.

Maggie started several other businesses, such as *The St. Luke Herald*, the Black American newspaper that raised awareness of the Order. Maggie promoted the establishment of a community center and programs to provide health care for African Americans.

In 1912 Maggie cofounded the Richmond Council of Colored Women, and she served as its president. The organization raised money for the support of Janie Porter Barrett's Industrial School for Colored Girls. Maggie was a member of the International Council of Women of the Darker Races, the National Association of Wage Earners, National Urban League and the Virginia Interracial Committee. She also helped found the Richmond Branch of the NAACP (National Association for the Advancement of Colored People).

Maggie Lena Walker's achievements enhanced the city of Richmond, as well as the people of Virginia. In her honor, the city government has named a street, a theater, and a high school after this celebrated woman. The house her family occupied from 1904 to 1934 is now the Maggie L. Walker National Historic Site.